The wonder of mothers

C. R. Gibson®

FINE GIFTS SINCE 1870

All images © Hulton Getty Picture Collection.
Picture research by Jon Wright.
Design by Keith Jackson.
All text, unless otherwise attributed, by Jonathan Bicknell.

Developed by Publishing Services Corporation, Nashville, Tennessee.

Published by C. R. Gibson®
C. R. Gibson® is a registered trademark of Thomas Nelson, Inc.
Nashville, Tennessee 37214
Printed and bound by L. Rex Printing Company Limited, China

ISBN 0-7667-6754-X
UPC 0-82272-46684-5
GB4151

The wonder of mothers

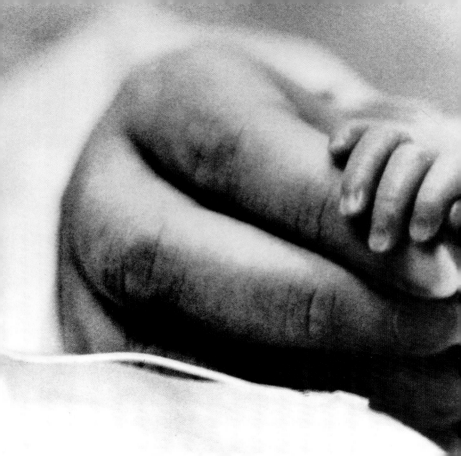

"To a **mother** is given the **priceless** gift of **life.**"

"Behind every successful woman stands a proud mother."

"Hand in Hand with the ones I love."

"Here's to the **happiest** years of our lives."

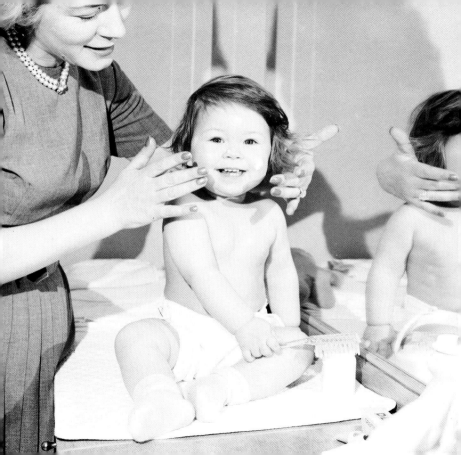

"Like
Mother,
like
Daughter."

"You were my world. And as I grew you showed me the universe."

"Safe from all harms, in the fold of your arms."

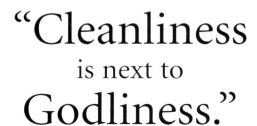

"Cleanliness
is next to
Godliness."

"Mother,
thanks for the
memories."

"No matter who they become, to a mother they are always children."

"You were
my eyes
and ears..."

"...and you were always there to hold me up."

"You did all the work, but always made it seem like a treat."

"And if **something** was there to be **enjoyed,** you always included me."

"I know whose prayers would make me whole, Mother, o'mine, O'Mother o'mine." – Rudyard Kipling